The GOLF Alphabet Book

by Stephanie S. Ellis

DEDICATED TO MY SON, MICHAEL VIENNE WHO STARTED PLAYING GOLF IN HIS THIRTIES AND BECAME A GOLF PRO BEFORE HE WAS FORTY.

TO ALL YOUNGSTERS WHO PLAY GOLF AND TO THE PARENTS AND COACHES WHO ENCOURAGE THEM IN THEIR SPORT.

Photo credits are Depositphotos.com

All rights reserved. This book, or parts thereof, may not be reproduced in any form without permission in writing from the publisher.

Library of Congress Cataloging-in-Publication Data
Ellis, Stephanie Shriber,
The GOLF Alphabet Book / Stephanie Shriber Ellis p 47
An overview of alphabetical terms and pictures pertaining to GOLF...
Paperback   ISBN 9780989811859
1. GOLF --- Juvenile literature [1. GOLF] 1. Title

Published in the United States by Mackenzie Woods Publishers
Printed in USA
First Edition 1

Mackenzie Woods Publishing
www.Mackenziewoodspublishing.com

FORE!

A

ALIGNMENT - ADDRESS POSITION

Alignment is the beginning position of your swing. To hit the ball straight to the target you must have your shoulders, hips and feet in a straight line. Your back should be straight as you bend from the hips with your knees slightly bent.

BACKSWING
The back swing is when you begin your swing by bringing the club back low and smooth.

B

C

CADDIES

Caddy is the person who carries a player's bag and clubs, and gives insightful advice and moral support. A good caddy is aware of the challenges and obstacles of the course being played.

CARTS

Golfers who don't want to carry their golf clubs or use a caddy, rent pull carts or motorized carts.

COURSES

An area of land laid out for the playing of golf with a series of 9 or 18 holes each including tee, fairway and putting green. They usually include one or more natural or artifical hazards.

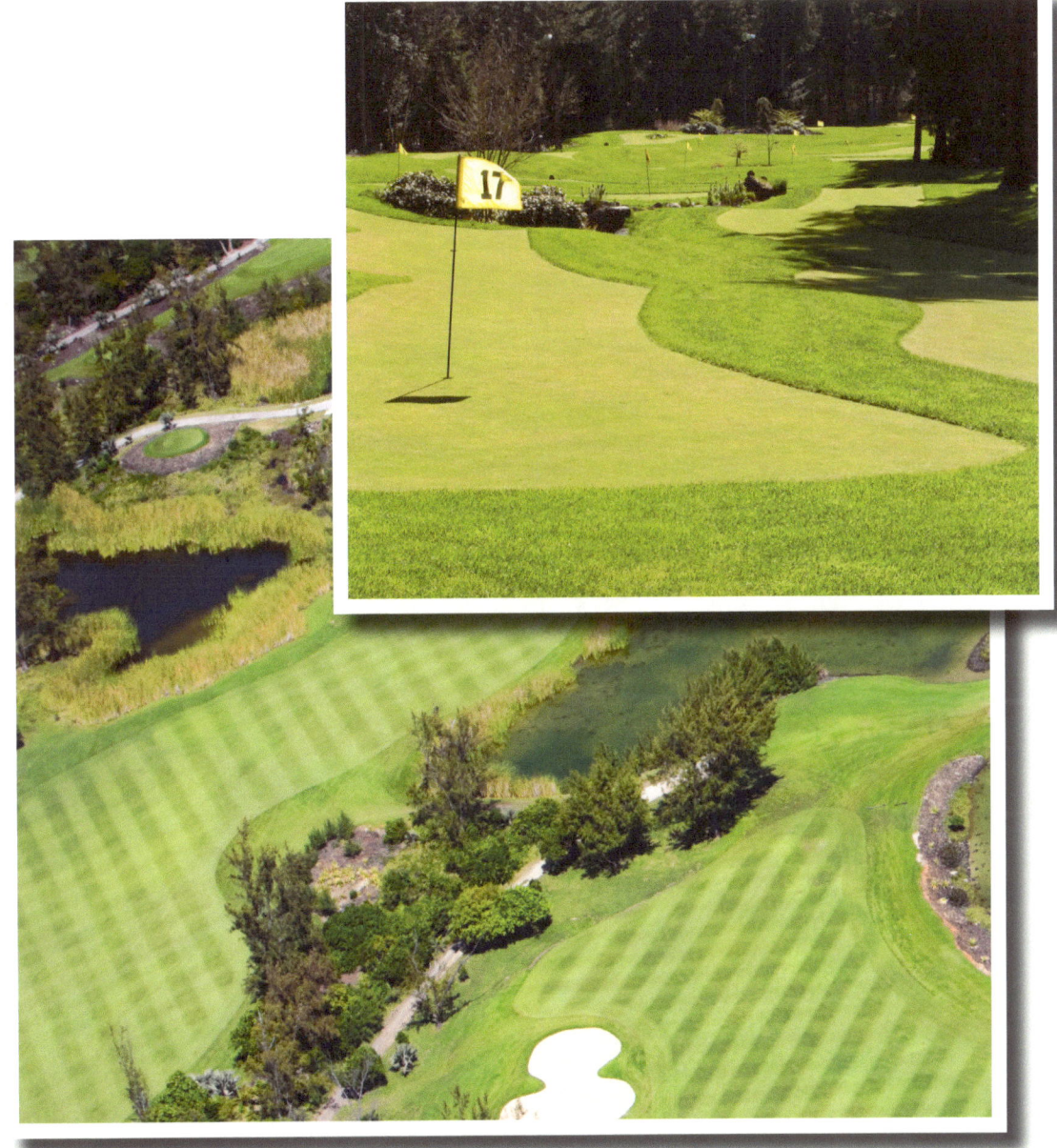

D DRIVING RANGE

This is the area set aside for players to practice their strokes with range balls.

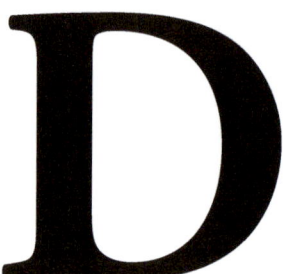

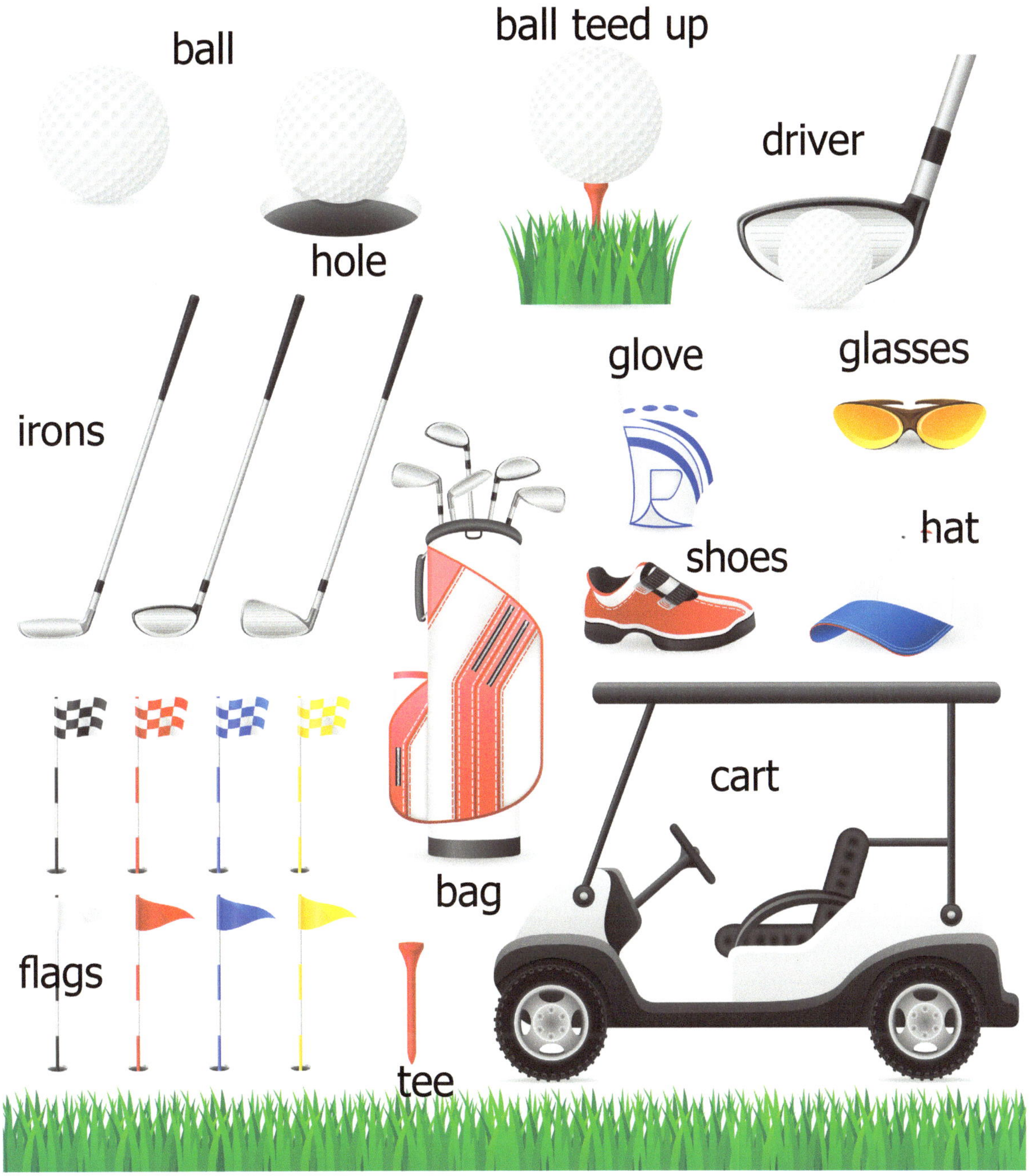

ball
ball teed up
driver
hole
glove
glasses
irons
shoes
hat
flags
bag
cart
tee

EQUIPMENT
All those things worn and used when playing the game of golf are called equipment.

FAIRWAY

The fairway is the closely mown area that usually runs between the tee box and putting green of a golf hole and is the target for golfers on all holes.

FULL SWING

In a full swing your feet are about shoulder width apart. Your back foot points straight out from your body while the front foot is turned slightly towards the hole.

GIMMIE

In golf, a gimmie is a shot that the other players agree can count automatically without being actually played. Usually a very short putt.

GRIP

There are several kinds of grips, the interlocking grip, the overlapping grip and the ten finger grip similar to the baseball grip.

G

GOLF ETIQUETTE

Etiquette is the application of good manners and concerns the courtesy that golfers show other golfers on the course. It is the most valued part of the game of golf and differs from other sports that rely on a referee to enforce rules and behavior. Each golfer is his own score keeper.

- It is proper etiquette to arrive on time and be properly dressed. The first thing to do is to check your equipment and be sure that you have everything that you need. It is smart to warm up on the practice range before beginning your play. The first tee will set the tone for the day.

- Safety is the first concern for all golfers. Be aware of other golfers that are around you when you take your first swing from any tee. Be sure to be behind the markers as teeing ahead of the markers is a penalty. Wait until everyone in your group has teed off before you head down the fairway.

- Respect for those around you is important. Keep your voice low with no loud noises to disturb others. Concentration is a large part of golf and those players around you should not be disturbed by loud noises. But if you hit a ball and it looks like it is headed towards another golfer, holler **"Fore"** as loud as you can. It is the one time that the quiet rule does not apply.

- It is courteous to allow faster players to play through if you are playing slower that usual or looking for a lost ball. If you are the first group out keep a good pace going. If there is a group in front of you don't hit until you know the group ahead is out of range.

- Replace any divots that you may cause in the fairways.

- Enter any bunkers the nearest to your ball and exit the same way. Remember to rake the bunker after play.

- Know where you can drive your cart and stay on the path. Pull carts must be kept off the greens.

- Remember that the greens are very delicate. Be careful not to damage them with your shoes, spikes or clubs.

- If your ball makes a mark when it hits the green use your ball-mark tool to repair it. When on the green, do not walk in front of another player's ball as you can make an indent.

- When a golfer is putting the flag must be removed from the hole and gently laid off the green. If a player has a long putt and trouble seeing the hole, another golfer can **tend the flagstick** for that golfer. He stands holding the flagstick at an arm's length from the hole, keeping the flag from flapping, making sure that his shadow does not fall across the hole. As the ball rolls towards the hole, the flagstick is removed and placed off the green.

- When your group is finished putting, carefully replace the flagstick and move off the green, proceed to the next tee and record your scores.

H HAZARDS

The hazards on a golf course can be natural or man-made. They consist of water, rivers or lakes, and sand bunkers.

Use a sand wedge to get out of a bunker.

IRONS

The irons are known as the workhorses of any golf bag and can help to lower your handicap. Learn what you can do with each iron. Each iron has a different loft angle.

JUMP FOR JOY
A hole in one!

K KEEPING SCORE

Each time you swing at the ball it counts as one stroke on your score, whether you are driving the ball down the fairway or putting on the green. Each player tallies his own score.

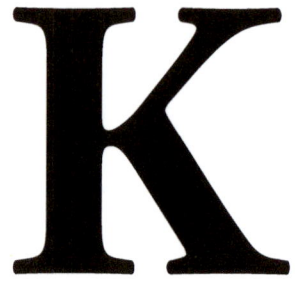

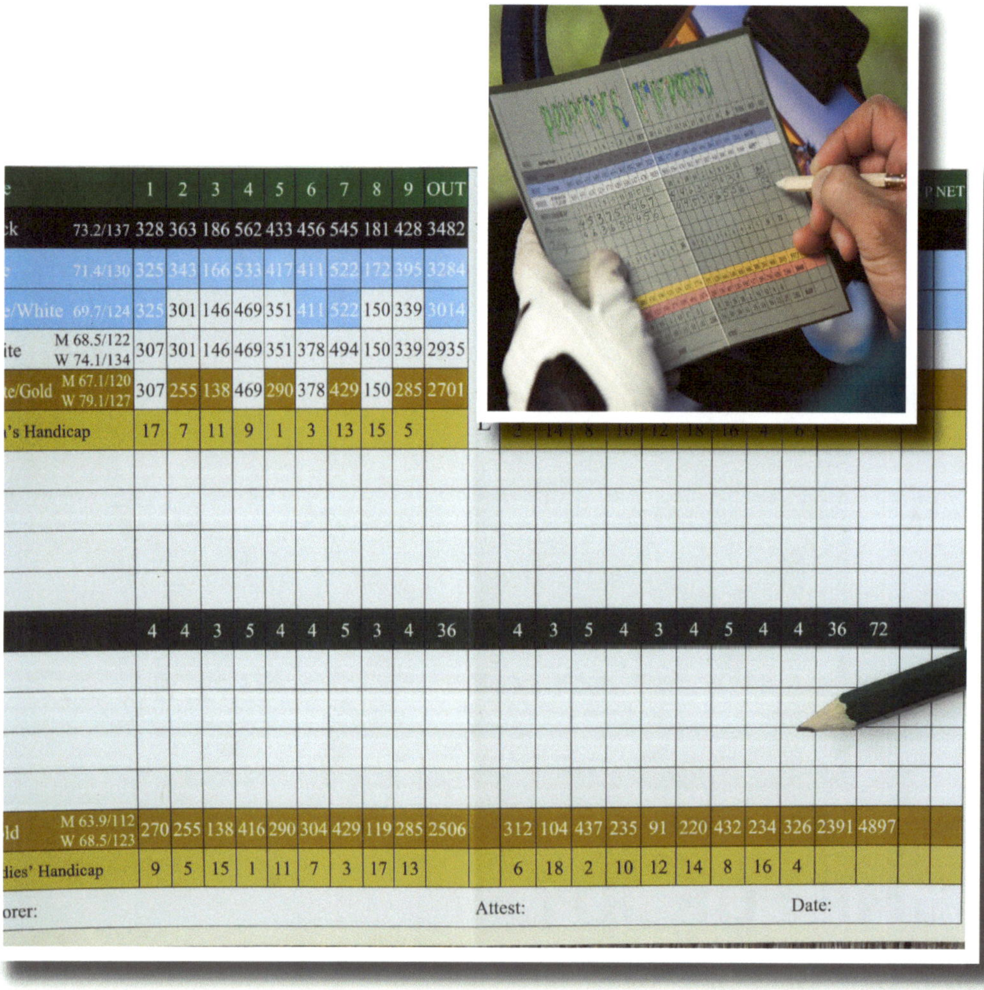

LOST BALL

If a ball cannot be found after searching for it for five minutes, a provisional ball may be put in play by teeing off from the spot where the lost ball was last hit. A lost ball causes an extra stroke to be added to your score.

LIE
The lie of the ball greatly influences your next stroke.

M MATCH PLAY

Unlike stroke play, in which the unit of scoring is the total number of strokes taken over one or more rounds of golf, match play scoring consists of individual holes won, halved or lost. On each hole, the most that can be gained is one point.

What grip do I use?

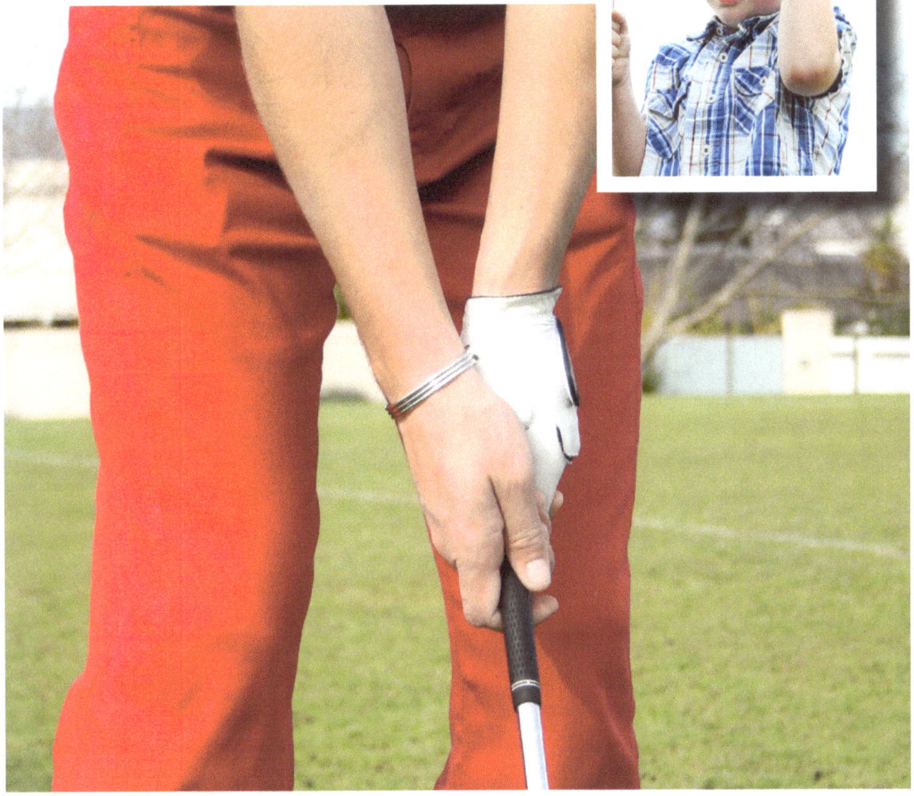

NATURAL GRIP

To use this grip, the golfer closes the fingers around the shaft so that his little finger touches the index finger of the left hand. The palm rests slightly to the right of the shaft and then covers the left thumb. This is called the natural grip.

O OUT OF BOUNDS

Any ball that is hit outside the boundaries is called "out of bounds" and costs the player a stroke.

If your shot sends the ball out of bounds, you must bring it back to where you hit it from and take a penalty stroke. If you cannot find your ball, go back to where you hit from, drop another ball and continue play. However you must add a penalty stroke to your score.

POSITION AND POSTURE

Position and posture are two terms which stress how you address the ball. It is important to have good balance in your swing and your club face and head should aim at the target.
[See Alignment]

PUTTING ON THE PRACTICE GREEN

There is an area set aside at golf courses called the putting green or practice green, where players can practice their putting. Good putting will make your game but bad putting will break your game. Practice your putting!

QUIET
A sign used at tournaments to remind the crowd that quiet is necessary while players are playing a ball.

R ROUGH

The rough is an area of grass not mowed alongside the fairway that punishes an off-line shot.

RULES OF THE GAME OF GOLF

The rules of golf, as written by the USGA , are based on players' honesty and integrity and the fun and fair play of the game. Every player of the game is his or her own referee. No one is abused but one's self, if the etiquette or the rules are broken.

Here are printed the basic rules and information for beginners to know when they begin the game. Further rules can be found in the USGA's offical Rule Book of Golf.

The golf course is divided into four zones: teeing grounds, hazards, putting greens and the rest of the course called "through the green".

- The rules of golf say that you can carry no more than 14 clubs in your golf bag, but starting out all you need to play are a 3 wood, 5 and 7 irons and a putter.
- Each hole starts with teeing off the teeing ground.
- Honors are who takes the first shot, determined by draw, flipping a coin or lot.
- When teeing off or hitting on the fairway, always watch your ball until it stops so you know where to find it when it is your turn to hit again.
- After teeing off, play continues with the player farthest back shooting next.
- During play, if the player moves the ball by accident or intentionally, he is awarded a one stroke penalty.
- You cannot improve the position of your ball by bending, or breaking anything fixed in front of your ball.
- If you lose your ball or hit it out of bounds, you must

drop another ball as close as possible to the spot from which your first ball was hit.
- You must count every swing you make, even if you miss the ball.
- You must play the ball from where it lands, unless it goes out of bounds or into the water. Then you must take a penalty shot and drop a new ball back where you hit the first ball from.
- Remember to always treat the bunkers with respect. If your ball is in a bunker enter at the place nearest to the ball, being careful not to hurt the edges of the bunker. Rake foot prints and any indentations that you have made before moving on.
- There is no penalty if your ball hits another ball or the flagstick when you are shooting to get on the green. Just replace the opponent's ball to as close a position as it was when you hit it.
- On the greens the farthest from the hole shoots first. Ask any player whose ball is in your line to mark his ball and remove it. It is a two stroke penalty to hit another's ball on the green when putting.
- Remove the flagstick before putting. It is a two stroke penalty if you hit the flagstick.
- After everyone in your group has putted out, replace the flagstick and leave the green for the next tee and record your score. This allows golfers behind you to move forward without delay.

Play with enthusiasm and have fun. Enjoy your day on the course. Golf is a lifetime sport.

S

SAND RAKE

SAND WEDGE

SANDTRAP

Sandtrap is an old name for what is now referred to as a bunker. Bunkers can be found anywhere on the course.

BUNKER

TEE

The Tee is a closely mown area from which the first stroke on a hole is played. A Tee is also a small wooden peg used to hold the ball up for hitting the ball.

TEEING UP

TEEING OFF

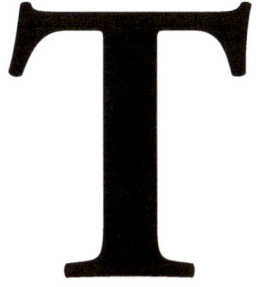

U

UNPLAYABLE LIE

An unplayable lie is when the golf ball lands in a position from which the golfer cannot take a shot.

VISUALIZATION
Visualization means seeing in your mind's eye what you want to happen.

VICTORY
Winning means Victory!

VOLUNTEER
Volunteers are the backbone of all sports and golf tournaments. They help with transportation, help the organizer with all his tasks and help by directing fans or visitors on the course.

V

W

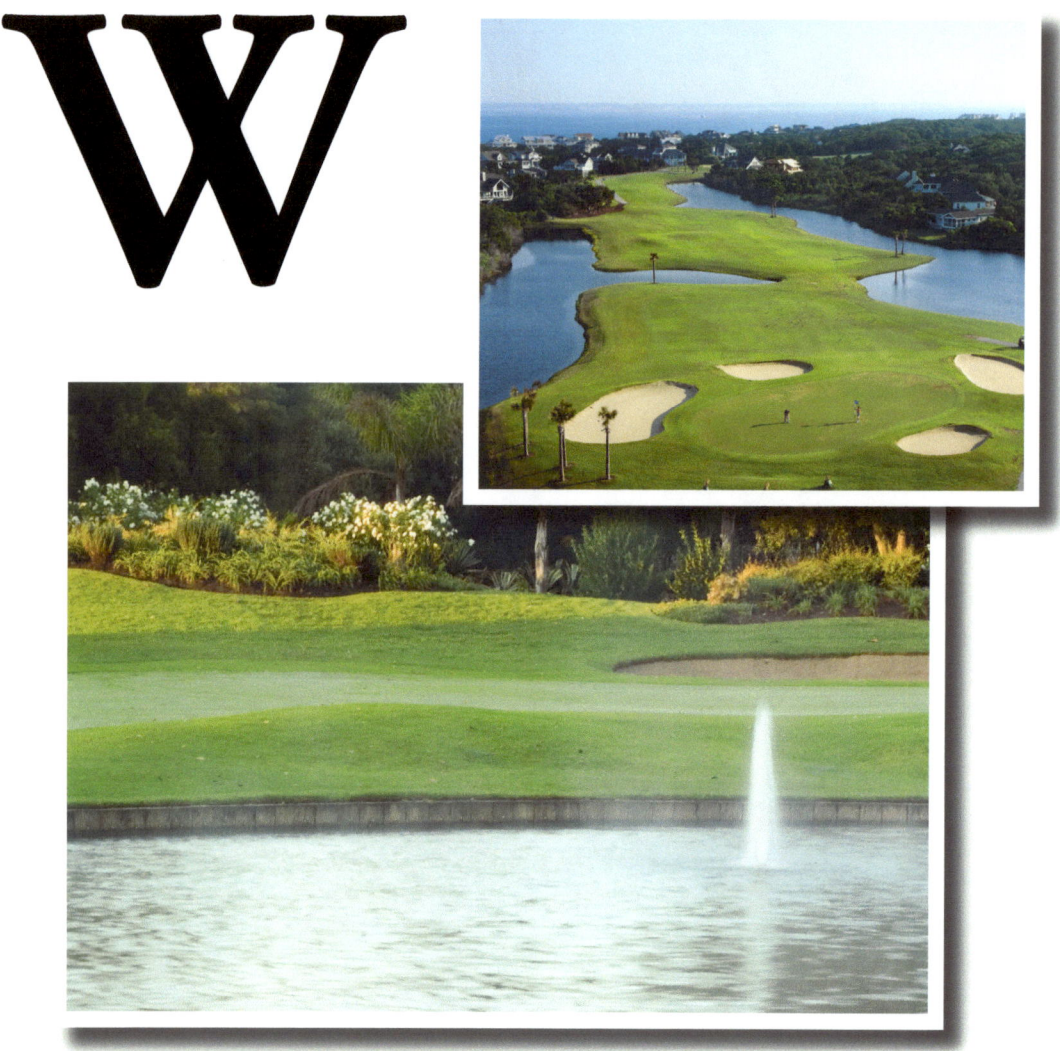

WATER HAZARD

Golf courses have lakes or rivers considered to be water hazards that players have to shoot around or over to get to the putting green. Upon entering the water hazard, if the ball is playable, they can play it, but if it is not they must take a penalty stroke and either take a drop or return to where they last hit the ball.

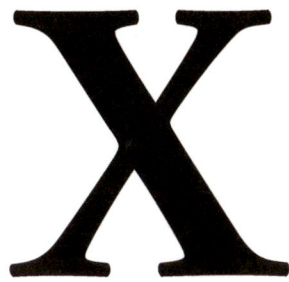

EXTRA STROKES

Extra strokes are another name for penalty strokes.

- A stroke is counted for a whiff, which is swinging at the ball and missing.

- If your ball goes in the water or trees where it is impossible to hit, you may pick up the ball and move it to an area not closer to the hole and continue to play it, but you must take a one penalty stroke.

- If you can't find your ball, add a penalty stroke and go back to where you shot from and hit again.

- If you bump your ball or it moves when you remove a twig from the fairway you must take a two stroke penalty.

- The player farthest from the hole putts first. If the opponent's ball is in the way you may ask him to mark it and remove it. Otherwise you will get a two stroke penalty if you hit his ball.

- If you do not remove the flag pole before sinking your putt, you will get a two stroke penalty.

Y

YELLOW STAKES
Yellow stakes are markers on a golf course indicating which area is designated as a water hazard. A seasonal creek may not have water in it but the stakes indicate it as a water hazard.

ZONE

There are different zones on a golf course known as the TEE Box, fairways, roughs, greens, water hazards, out of bounds and bunkers. All are maintained on a regular basis by the maintenance crew with different equipment.

GLOSSARY

ADDRESS POSITION - The position the golfer takes when he is ready to hit the ball. It includes his posture, stance, and grip.

AERATE THE GREENS - To infuse or force air into the greens. Without aeration the greens die.

ALIGNMENT- The club face must be aimed at the target and the alignment of the body must match the angle of the club face.

APPROACH - Shot played to the Green from the Fairway.

APRON - The narrow area surrounding the green which is cut shorter than the fairway but longer than the green.

AWAY - Refers to who is farthest away from the pin.

BACK NINE - The second nine holes of a golf course.

BACK SWING - the first part of the golf swing that takes the club back and prepares to hit the ball.

BIRDIE - A term used in scoring which means one under the par for the hole.

BOGEY - A term used in scoring for one over the par for the hole.

BREAK - A term for the amount that a putt will deviate from the straight line due to the slope of the putting green.

BUNKER - A hazard on the course which is filled with sand. Previously called a sand trap.

BUNKER SHOT - A shot to get out of the bunker.

CADDIES - Those individuals who can be hired to carry bags and clubs for players.

CARRY - The distance a ball has to fly to get over a hazard.

CHIP SHOT - A short shot intended to get the ball on the green. Normally played from near the edge of the green towards the hole.

CUP - A name for the hole on the green where the flagstick is located.

DIMPLES - Are the indentations on the golf ball.

DIVOT - A clump of grass that has been removed by the club-head when the shot is made.

DOGLEG - The bend in the fairway changing direction, turning to the left or right.

DOUBLE EAGLE - Term used to describe three under par.

DRAW - A stroke deliberately played with right to left spin, which causes the ball to curve from right to left in its flight.

DRIVER - A number one wood usually used to tee off for maximum distance.

DRIVING RANGE - An area where players can practice their shots.

DROP - Ball that is put back into play using specific rules that guide how to drop it.

EAGLE - A score in golf that is two strokes under par on a hole.

EQUIPMENT - Those things used by a golfer to play the game; the machinery used to maintain the course and greens.

FADE - A stoke with a left to right spin that causes the ball to curve from left to right in its flight.

FAIRWAY - An area of closely mown grass between the TEE and the Green.

FLAGSTICKS - Flags set in the cup to show where the hole is.

FOLLOW THROUGH - The final part of the golf swing, in which the golfer turns towards the target and brings his hands up over his shoulders.

FORE - A warning cry to warn golfers that a ball hit at high speed is coming towards them.

FOREWARD SWING - the part of the golf swing that starts at the top of the back swing and goes to the finish.

FRONT NINE - The first nine holes on a golf course.

GIMMIE - A short putt which does not have to be played out, given by the opponent. The stroke is not taken but a stroke counts to the score.

GOLF ETIQUETTE - The code of proper behavior and courtesies that golfers extend to each other when playing on the golf course.

GREEN - At the end of each hole there is an area of short grass with a small hole. You are trying to get into that hole with as few strokes as possible.

GRIP - How you hold the club.

HANDICAP - A rating system for golfers to determine their level of play.

HAZARD - A hazard is a place on the golf course which creates problems for the golfer during their effort to reach the greens.

HEAD - The end of the golf club which strikes the ball.

HEEL - The part at the base of the shaft and closest to the golfer.

HOLE - A general term regarding the area from the Tee to the green; also referred to the hole on the green where the flagstick resides.

HOLE IN ONE- Getting the ball into the hole with one stroke.

HOOK - Stroke that bends the ball sharply to the left.

IMPACT - The moment the ball is hit.

INTERLOCKING GRIP - A way of gripping the handle of the club where the little finger of the right hand intertwines with the forefinger of the left hand. [opposite applies to a left handed player].

IRONS - set of clubs with metal heads graduated in loft to give different flight to the ball when hit.

LAG PUTT - A long putt to get the ball as close to the flagstick as you can so that you can sink it easily on your next turn.

LAY UP - A lay up is when a golfer hits a short shot up to a hazard in hopes of being able to get over the hazard with his next shot.

LIE - The position of your ball on the ground and how it pertains to the kind of shot you can make.

LIPPED OUT - A ball that went around the lip of the hole and rolled away.

LPGA - Ladies Professional Golf Association.

LOFT - Angle and slope of the face of the club.

MATCH PLAY - Form of competition in which the number of holes won or lost by a player or team, rather than the number of strokes taken, determines the winner.

MULLIGAN - When you get to take a bad shot over. Never allowed in a tournament.

OUT OF BOUNDS - The area of a golf course designated to be beyond the playing area and marked by white stakes.

PAR - the score that an expert golfer would be expected to make on a given hole.

PGA - Professional Golf Association

PITCHING WEDGE - A club with more loft than a 9 - iron.

PROVISIONAL BALL - A ball played in place of one that may be lost.

PUTTER - A golf club with little loft that is designed to roll the ball to the hole.

PENALTY STROKE - Stroke given as a penalty for rules broken.

READ THE GREEN - Determining which way the ball will roll across the greens on its way to the hole.

ROUGH - The area that runs parallel to the fairway where the grass is allowed to grow longer than the fairway.

ROUND - A game or round of golf is nine or eighteen holes.

SAND TRAP - Another name for bunker.

SAND WEDGE - A club with a high loft that is used to hit balls out of a bunker.

SCORE CARD - A score card which contains information about the course, local rules and distances to holes is provided by the golf course. It is used to keep your individual score for each hole.

SCRATCH GOLFER - A golfer who has a zero handicap.

SHAFT- The long, thin part of the club that joins the head of the club to the grip.

SHOES - Golf shoes normally have spikes in the soles to help the golfer grip the ground better when hitting a ball.

SKY BALL - A miss hit shot which is hit very high and with no forward distance.

SLICE - When struck by a right handed golfer, the ball curves considerably far to the right.

STANCE - This is the overall body position of a golfer as he addresses the golf ball.

STROKE AND DISTANCE - The penalty for an out of bounds shot in golf; the golfer must take a penalty stroke and hit again from the place where the ball was originally hit before it went out of bounds.

SWEET SPOT - Precise point on the face of the club which will make a ball travel farther than one struck on any other part of the club.

TEE - Closely mown area where the first stroke on a hole is made. The wood peg on which a ball is placed to tee off.

TEEING GROUND - The teeing ground is an area of short grass with markers to show you where to hit from.

TEMPO - The speed at which a golfer swings a golf club.

TEND THE FLAGPOLE - To remove the flagstick for other golfers in the group.

TEN FINGERED GRIP - an interlocking of fingers to hold the club shaft.

TOPPED - Stroke in which the club strikes the top of the ball, causing it to run along the ground.

TOUCH - If you have the right touch when putting, you have the right and proper amount of force for the shot required.

TOURNAMENT RULE SHEET TRIPLE BOGEY - A unit of score meaning three strokes over par.

TURN - The end of the front nine and going into the back nine.

UNPLAYABLE LIE - When the golf ball lands in a spot that is impossible to play or stroke, it is called an unplayable lie.

USGA - United States Golf Association

VOLUNTEER - A person who volunteers their time and energy to help.

WATER HAZARD - Many golf courses have rivers or lakes which the golfer must go by or over. These are considered hazards.

WHIFF - To swing and miss.

WHITE STAKES - designates out of bounds areas.

WOODS - can be an area of dense trees where the golfer does not want to hit into. Also the three woods used in driving the ball.

WRONG BALL - Refers to playing the ball that was not yours to be played.

YARDAGE - The distance from Tee to Green is so many yards and marked at the beginning of each hole.

YELLOW STAKES - used to mark hazard areas on the course such as water.

ZONE - The golf course is divided into the tee ground, fairways, greens and hazards.

Other books written by Stephanie S. Ellis

- **MY PERSONAL SOCCER JOURNAL**
  An Educational Guide and Scrapbook for Children and Parents

- **The SOCCER Alphabet Book**
- **The BASEBALL Alphabet Book**
- **The TENNIS Alphabet book**

www.soccerpals.com
www.mackenziewoodspublishing.com

Stephanie Shriber Ellis always wanted to work with children and started her career as an early Elementary school teacher, in Lakewood, Ohio. She later taught in Erie, Pennsylvania where she opened the first private licensed Nursery school in the State.

She began writing books for children to help them develop a better understanding of the different terms connected with the sports they play and be able to feel comfortable utilizing them.

Using photographs with the alphabet letters, her books are a great introductory start to either tennis, soccer, baseball or the golf language. The books are fun, and inviting educational resources for children from six to twelve years of age. They help coach the children to discover the ins and outs of the sport regardless of when they begin to play.

Ms. Ellis lives in Florida with her family, two dogs and three feisty cats.

www.ingramcontent.com/pod-product-compliance
Lightning Source LLC
Chambersburg PA
CBHW041535040426
42446CB00002B/95